MY FIRST YEAR

A BEATRIX POTTER BABY BOOK ™

F. WARNE & CO.

FREDERICK WARNE
Published by the Penguin Group, 27 Wrights Lane, London W8 5TZ, England
Penguin Books USA Inc., 375 Hudson Street, New York, New York 10014, USA
Penguin Books Australia Ltd, Ringwood, Victoria, Australia
Penguin Books Canada Ltd, 10 Alcorn Avenue, Toronto, Ontario, Canada M4V 3B2
Penguin Books (N.Z.) Ltd, 182-190 Wairau Road, Auckland 10, New Zealand

Penguin Books Ltd, Registered Offices: Harmondsworth, Middlesex, England

This new edition published 1998 by Frederick Warne
3 5 7 9 10 8 6 4 2
Original concept and title devised by Judy Taylor for first edition 1983

ISBN 0 7232 4380 8

Printed and bound in Great Britain by William Clowes Limited, Beccles and London

THE KEEPSAKE POCKET

In the back of this book, there is a pocket where you can store precious mementos. The first few months after your baby's arrival are busy ones and you may not always have time to update this journal as regularly as you would like. Instead, you may find it easier to make rough notes in your spare time, and store them in the keepsake pocket, along with your prenatal scans, and favourite photographs (remember to write the date and a brief comment on the back). You may also like to keep a lock of your baby's hair, your first Mother's Day card, or other special items in the keepsake pocket.

ABOUT MY PARENTS

My parents just before I was born

My mother's name   My father's name

WAITING FOR ME

IDEAS FOR NAMES

Boys' names

Girls' names

My prenatal scans

My parents' feelings about my arrival

My Arrival

My name is

_____

I was born on   at

_____

I weighed   I measured (length)

_____

My eyes were   My hair was

_____

The midwife's name was   The doctor's name was

_____

My first picture

MY BIRTH STORY

My hospital bracelet

My birth

_____

_____

_____

_____

My parents' feelings when I arrived

_____

_____

_____

_____

MY FIRST FEW DAYS

Me arriving at home

My visitors

_____

_____

_____

_____

_____

_____

_____

Settling In

I came home on

_____

My First Night

I fell asleep at

_____

I fell asleep at

_____

I fell asleep at

_____

I woke up at

_____

I woke up again at

_____

I woke up yet again at

_____

My sleeping patterns in my first week

_____

_____

My feeding patterns in my first week

_____

_____

My parents' first impressions

_____

_____

_____

MY HANDS AND FEET

My hand and footprints at two weeks

Gifts, Cards and Flowers

A Record

ABOUT MY NAME

Photograph of me at (age)

My name means   My name was chosen by

The reason why my name was chosen

My Family Tree

Great Grandparents	Great Grandparents	Great Grandparents	Great Grandparents

Grandfather	Grandmother	Grandfather	Grandmother

Aunts/Uncles	Mother	Father	Aunts/Uncles

Brothers   Me   Sisters

Moving Around

Use this page to record special moments as your baby grows more independent

	DATE	AGE
I lifted my head		
I 'found' my hands		
I rolled over		
I sat with support		
I sat alone		
I moved around or crawled		
I pulled myself up		
I took my first steps		

Photograph of me crawling

TALKING

*Use this page to record special moments as
your baby communicates with you*

My first smile

	DATE	AGE
I smiled		
I laughed		
I babbled		
I copied noises		
I started 'singing'		
I started understanding words		

FAMILY AND FRIENDS

Use these pages to record special moments as your baby gets to know friends and family

I moved my eyes to watch you (date)

_____

at (weeks/months)

_____

Comments

_____

_____

_____

_____

I smiled for special people (date)   at (weeks/months)

_____   _____

Comments

_____   _____

I cried when you left (date)   at (weeks/months)

_____   _____

Comments

_____   _____

_____   _____

A photograph of me with

_____

I said your name (date)   at (weeks/months)

_____   _____

Comments

_____

_____

I cuddled you (date)   at (weeks/months)

_____   _____

Comments

_____

_____

FIRST EXPERIENCES

Use these pages to describe unforgettable outings
as your baby begins to explore the world

I first went swimming (date)   at (weeks/months)

Comments

I first went to the playground (date)   at (weeks/months)

Comments

I went to my first party (date)

at (weeks/months)

Comments

I went on my first holiday (date)

at (weeks/months)

Comments

Me on holiday

I wore my first pair of shoes (date)   at (weeks/months)

Comments

I had my first haircut (date)   at (weeks/months)

Comments

SPECIAL OCCASIONS

*Use these pages to mark religious festivals, special naming
ceremonies or celebrations in the first year*

MEALTIMES

I was first weaned from the
breast/bottle (date)

_____

at (weeks/months)

_____

Comments

_____

_____

_____

_____

I tried my first solids (date)   at (weeks/months)

_____

Comments

_____

_____

I tried puréed food (date)   at (weeks/months)

_____

Comments

_____

_____

DATE AGE

I tried chopped food _____ _____

I tried finger food _____ _____

I first held a spoon _____ _____

I fed myself _____ _____

I drank from a beaker _____ _____

My favourite foods

_____

_____

_____

_____

My least favourite foods

_____

_____

_____

A photograph of me in my highchair

Bathtime

Me in the baby bath

My favourite bath toys

_____

_____

_____

_____

_____

Games in the bath

_____

_____

_____

_____

Me in the big bath

BEDTIME

Bedtimes change as babies grow up. Use these pages to help you record bedtimes in the first year

My bedtime is at

Date (weeks/months)

Evening routines in the first year

I moved to a cot (date)   at (weeks/months)

Comments

I slept through the night (date)   at (weeks/months)

Comments

My favourite books, toys
and lullabies at bedtime

_____

_____

_____

_____

_____

_____

_____

_____

Me in my pyjamas

Night-time habits

_____

_____

_____

_____

PLAYING GAMES

Use these pages to help you record
what made your baby laugh

First games *(Boo!, pulling faces, hide and seek, bouncing on the bed, chase . . .)*

Things that make me laugh

Me playing one of my favourite games

My favourite toys

Me with one of my favourite toys

My favourite songs

MY HEALTH

Immunisations	DATE	AGE
Eyesight tests		
Hearing tests		
Childhood illnesses		
Allergies		
Blood group		
Doctor		

MY TEETH

The first tooth can appear at any time in the first or second year.
When the first tooth appears, write in the date next to number 1
on the list below. Then number the relevant tooth in the diagram, and so on.

DATE

1 _____

2 _____

3 _____

4 _____

5 _____

6 _____

7 _____

8 _____

9 _____

10 _____

Upper

Right

Left

Lower

DATE

11 _____

12 _____

13 _____

14 _____

15 _____

16 _____

17 _____

18 _____

19 _____

20 _____

Some babies find teething a struggle, some hardly notice. This is how I behaved while I was teething.

_____

_____

_____

_____

_____

MY BABY RECORD
THREE MONTHS

Me at three months

Weight   Length

_____   _____

Feeding habits

_____

Sleeping pattern

_____

Comments

_____

_____

_____

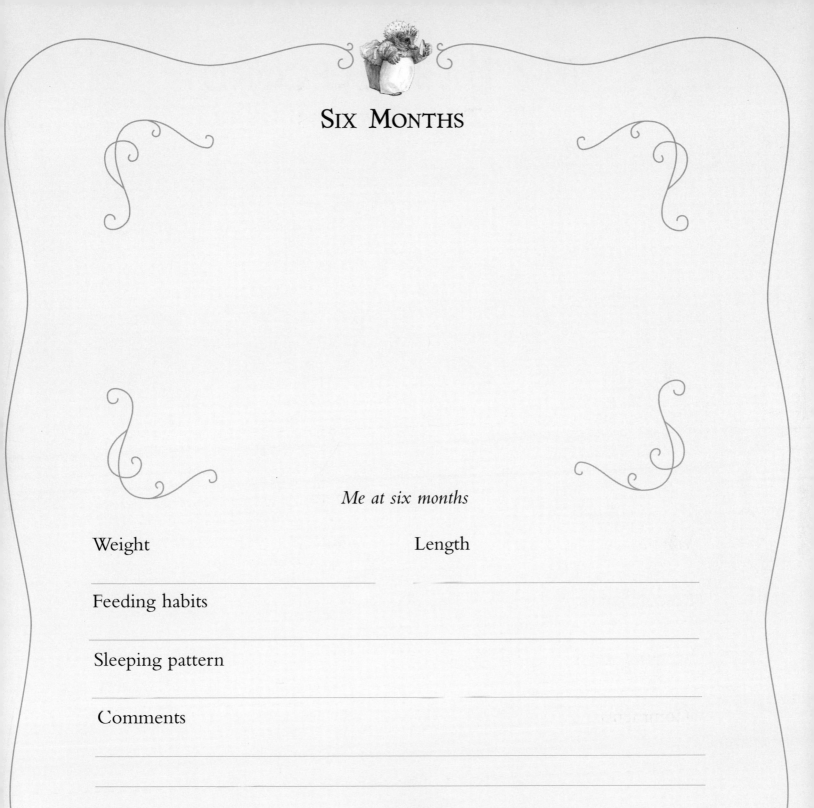

SIX MONTHS

Me at six months

Weight   Length

_____

Feeding habits

_____

Sleeping pattern

_____

Comments

_____

_____

_____

MY BABY RECORD
NINE MONTHS

Me at nine months

Weight

Length

Feeding habits

Sleeping pattern

Comments

Twelve Months

Me at twelve months

Weight   Length

Feeding habits

Sleeping pattern

Comments

MY HANDS AND FEET

My hand and footprints at one year

ARTISTIC TALENTS

My first scribble

MY FIRST BIRTHDAY

Me on my first birthday

Description of the day

_____

_____

_____

_____

Presents

_____

_____

_____

_____

_____

_____

_____

_____

_____

_____

Who visited

_____

_____

_____

_____

My birthday cake *(who bought or made it, and what it looked like)*

_____

_____

_____

_____

THE END OF MY FIRST YEAR

Comments *(my parents' feelings, and a summary of the last twelve months)*

_____

_____

_____

_____

_____

_____